MORE
BUCKS
ANNUALLY

MORE
BUCKS
ANNUALLY

Insider's Guide
to Getting Your MBA,
DBA, and PhD Online

Dr. Ken K. Wong

U21Global Graduate School | University of Toronto

iUniverse, Inc.
Bloomington

MORE BUCKS ANNUALLY

Insider's Guide to Getting Your MBA, DBA, and PhD Online

iUniverse books may be ordered through booksellers or by contacting:

iUniverse
1663 Liberty Drive
Bloomington, IN 47403
www.iuniverse.com
1-800-Authors (1-800-288-4677)

ISBN: 978-1-4620-0022-7 (pbk)
ISBN: 978-1-4620-0023-4 (ebk)

Printed in the United States of America
iUniverse rev. date: 2/22/11

To my wife Winnie, and my family members
Hello Ma, Hello Dad, and Hello Chiu

Thank you for your love, understanding, patience, and confidence.

About the Author

Dr. Ken Kwong-Kay Wong

Dr. Ken K. Wong is a U21 Global Marketing Professor and Subject Area Coordinator, training corporate executives and MBA students from over 70 countries. In 2008 and 2009, he received the Faculty Excellence Award, and was honoured in all three award categories, including: Outstanding Professor, Most Innovative Professor and Excellence in Online Education. Since 2003, Dr. Wong has been developing and lecturing marketing courses at the University of Toronto's School of Continuing Studies and also at various institutions of higher education in North America.

Dr. Wong's research interests include marketing for luxury brands, customer relationship management and online education. His articles have appeared in peer-reviewed international journals such as *Telecommunications Policy, Service Industries Journal,* and *Journal of Database Marketing and Customer Strategy Management.* Dr. Wong is also the author of the SCS lecture series in the areas of International Marketing, Advertising, PR & Publicity, E-Business, and Retail

Merchandising. His latest work includes *Approved Marketing Plans for New Products and Services, Avoiding Plagiarism, Discovering Marketing in 38 Hours, Putting a Stake in the Ground,* and *CRM in Action.*

Prior to entering the academic field, Dr. Wong was the Vice President of Marketing at TeraGo Networks (TSX: TGO) and had previously served as Director of eProduct Marketing at the e-commerce division of PSINet (NASDAQ: PSIX). He had also carried progressive product marketing roles at Sprint Canada and TELUS Mobility.

Certified by the American Marketing Association as a Professional Certified Marketer, Dr. Wong completed his Bachelor of Science degree at the University of Toronto and holds the International MBA degree from Nyenrode Business Universiteit in the Netherlands. He earned his Doctor of Business Administration degree from the University of Newcastle, Australia and has completed executive education programmes at both Kellogg and Queen's.

Table of Contents

Foreword

More Bucks Annually by Dr. Ken K. Wong is a wonderful new book that frankly addresses issues of business school learners around the globe. Dr. Wong has had an illustrious career as a professor, scholar, consultant in the areas of business, more specifically, in marketing; however, I know Dr. Wong as a colleague and outstanding professor to students around the globe. A major component of the life of academe is the transferrable knowledge imparted by professors to others; this book is just such a text.

More Bucks Annually provides invaluable information to any learner choosing to pursue a higher education degree beyond the Bachelors in the area of business; however, any learner choosing to consider higher degrees would do well to explore the content of the text. The information provided on professors and their credentials, the accreditation process, the value of an online education and especially the personal assessment of who one is, their preferred learning styles, and essential questions to ask — go far beyond just a degree in business. There is a wisdom that emerges as one peruses the text. From the structure to the conclusion of the book, one feels that Dr. Wong is sharing a narrative about exploring who one is in their search to be more than he or she has been in the past.

For those of you just beginning your graduate academic journey, the text leads you down a path of discovery to define and discern what truly matters in your decision making process. For those of you who have taken part of the journey and sense that your approach has been ill-planned, the text provide strategies for assessing how your decision was made with appropriate information for altering the path to more effectively respond to your desires and needs.

There are some wonderful jewels that need to be identified explicitly for each of you choosing to read this wonderful text:

- The first set of jewels is Dr. Wong's discussion of the pedagogical styles in online learning. Textbook-based programmes, Discussion board—based programmes, Research paper—based programmes, Proctor examination—based programmes, Facebook-based programmes, and Content enhanced-based programmes represent the landscape of online educational processes – but the true value of understanding the landscape is understanding yourself. Dr. Wong is intentional in guiding you to make the best-informed choice regarding who you are and how you connect with your learning.

- The second set of jewels is the section on the essential questions to ask. Too often, we enter new experiences in our lives ill-prepared and ill-advised regarding WHAT to ask, or HOW to explore what is necessary for the journey on which we are embarking. Knowing what is expected of you as a learner, how much it costs in tuition, books, student fees, and other factors can effectually shift your decision regarding where one might choose to attend a programme.

- The third set of jewels is the very frank discussion on the legitimacy of the institution where you choose to seek your advanced degree. There are so many schools in existence; but only certain schools will give you the "bang for your dollar". This is equally an issue for faculty choosing to enter online educational programmes as a professor/facilitator.

- The fourth set of jewels is the concern for accreditation. For example, Dr. Wong teaches at U21Global Graduate School — a member of AACSB and the only EFMD-CEL accredited online educational institution in the world. This school has attained the highest accreditation in Business Education, similar to the accreditations of Yale, Harvard, University of California - Berkeley, Stanford, and the Wharton School of

Business. So one can see that while accreditation is important – the type of accreditation can be most important for your career advancement purposes.

There are many additional jewels as one reads this text. For me, reading the text has provided new information for "this older scholar" and the information (for example, the Facebook-based programme) has already been useful in advising current learners regarding their choices for the future (I wish I could have given them a copy).

So what would I share with you about this text? Choosing the right educational program, pedagogical process, appropriately accredited institution for the journey of an MBA, DBA or PhD in the field of business is essential. Exploring options of Marketing, Strategy, Human Resources, Decision Theory, Organizational Behavior and so many more fields is part of the journey you take in matching who you are, what you value, how you learn, when you study, and where you choose to land in the exploration process. This text makes that journey so much easier!!!

Enjoy the reading!!! It is well worth the time.

Lloyd C. Williams, Ph.D., D.Min.

Former Provost, Northcentral University

CEO, The Institute for Transformative Thought and Learning

Preface

Since the financial crisis of 2008, many Canadians have been heading back to school to pursue further studies. However, the idea of leaving family members behind to study in a full-time graduate degree programme in another city seems to be a bad idea for many people. Even if the programme is offered in town, busy working professionals like you may find it virtually impossible to take night classes that typically start at 6pm in the downtown area.

The rapid deployment of broadband Internet infrastructure in Canada during the mid-2000s has made online education feasible to a lot of Canadians, whether they are residing in a densely populated metropolitan area or in a small town with just a few thousand people. That said, Canada is still way behind other developed countries such as the United States, the United Kingdom, and Australia in terms of embracing online education. Although our Athabasca University has been a pioneer in distance education since the 1970s, the concept of online education is still foreign to many Canadians. There is a general lack of government-run online degree programmes in Canada, and our first online doctoral programme still has a short-term residency requirement. This is in contrast to the development in other parts of the world in which one can study 100% online from high school all the way up to a PhD degree remotely at home.

The idea of writing this book was triggered by three major factors. First of all, more and more of my students are asking me to comment on those less-than-wonderful universities as they are attracted by some misleading marketing campaigns on the web. Some students almost fall into the trap of diploma mills. Hence, I sense an urgent need to help them in the university selection process. Second, students keep asking me about the "cheapest MBA" or the "fastest MBA" programme out there, without realizing that they should be more concerned about the university's reputation, the programme's pedagogy, and most importantly their objectives in pursuing a graduate business degree. I want to show my students the right kind of questions they should be asking about their degree. Finally, some of my MBA students are interested in pursuing an online DBA degree after graduation. Since there exist little resources about these newly launched doctoral programmes on the market, I hope this book can fill the knowledge gap in the Canadian market and guide these students to the right direction. As a professor who has taught online programmes for several years, and who also completed a 100% online DBA degree, I think I have some good tips to share with the readers.

Although many of my students and colleagues have reviewed the materials presented in this book, I know it is not perfect and is, in fact, far from perfect. As a writer, I would welcome your feedback on my work. Your suggestions will help shape future editions of this book, so don't feel shy to drop me an e-mail.

Dr. Ken K. Wong　黃廣基 博士

Ottawa, Ontario, Canada

January 30, 2011

e-mail: ken.wong@utoronto.ca

e-mail: kwong@u21global.edu.sg

Twitter: http://twitter.com/drkenkwong

Web: http://www.introductiontomarketing.ca

Acknowledgement

In completing my book, I have drawn support from many people and thus feel a huge debt of gratitude. I would like to thank the International Editorial Board for providing me with valuable input and constructive criticism to my work.

International Editorial Board:

Abdalla Gholoum
Annie Nyet Ngo Chan
Basil Pathrose
Chee Wai Hoo
Dutta Bholanath
Ekaterina Leonova
Engelbert Atangana
LH Kho
Khurshid Jussawalla
Kishore Pai
Lothar R. Pehl
Narendra Nesarikar
Rajen Kumar Shah
Richard Anthony
Shama Dewji
Tasneem Tailor
Vicky Yan Xu
Vien Cortes
Zulfikar Jiffry

Chapter 1 - Introduction

Pursue Your Educational Dreams

Just like many industries, the education sector in Canada is undergoing a paradigm shift. While traditional colleges and universities will not become obsolete tomorrow, an increasing number of Canadians are choosing the online learning route, and this spans from high school education all the way up to a doctoral programme. In my opinion, it is a good development because online education opens the door to those who may not otherwise have the opportunity to study, such as busy executives, students residing in remote areas, and those who may be physically challenged.

According to Canadian Virtual University (http://www.cvu-uvc.ca), the association of Canada's leading universities in online and distance education, over 300 online programmes are offered by universities across Canada. In addition, hundreds of online degree programmes are made available to Canadians by foreign universities. The bottom line is that online education is not a myth anymore. This innovative learning approach is gaining mainstream acceptance as more and more Canadians are earning their university degrees online.

Dr. Ken K. Wong

Online Education Is Eco-friendly

There are many benefits to online education. Flexibility and affordability are among the well-cited reasons why students are studying online. To the environmentalists, online education has another benefit – carbon footprint reduction. The elimination of paper-based assignments and the reduced use of traditional textbooks in online education definitely save lots of trees. Unlike an on-campus lecture, teaching online does not require professors to print tons of lecture notes for their students. Furthermore, online students do not need to drive their cars to campus. The savings on gasoline and pollutant emissions can be substantial.

To demonstrate the financial benefits of taking online classes, the State University of New York (SUNY) even created an "Online Learning Cost Savings Calculator" to show you the savings. This funny tool can be accessed at http://sln.suny.edu/gs/gs_costcalculator.shtml

Although recent research has indicated that surfing online may actually lead to CO_2 emissions (some even claimed that a Google search may generate up to 10g of CO_2), I think the benefits of online education outweigh its drawbacks (if any) from the environmental perspective.

Resistance to Online Education

As a marketing professor who has been teaching online MBA programmes for several years, I have often been asked if I had ever come across any resistance to online education. Frankly speaking, I would be lying if I said "No". The concerns of students are mainly related to the use of technology as many of them are baby boomers who are not that tech-savvy. However, once they have had the opportunity to give online classes a try, most of them would say "Ahh...That's easy and manageable!"

Where employers are concerned, the resistance to online education has dropped significantly in the past few years as this mode of education has started to enter the mainstream. With a growing number of world-renowned universities launching their own online degree programmes, and with business school accrediting agencies such as the European Foundation for Management Development (EFMD) now having a separate category of accreditation for "teChnology-Enhanced Learning (CEL) programmes", the reputation of online education has improved quite a bit in recent years. In the mid-2000s, the United Kingdom's *Financial Times* started to publish a separate list of the world's top online MBA programmes in addition to its annual business university rankings.

The Difference between Online and On-campus Study

Before getting too excited about online education, you should consider its unique pedagogical approach and determine if it fits your own learning style. For example, the way you socialize with others can be very different between the online and the face-to-face learning environments. In a traditional classroom setting, students can easily talk to each other and have lots of real-time interaction with classmates, the teaching assistant, and the professor. If you have a specific homework question, you can visit your professor during his or her office hours. When it comes to group projects, you may get together with other classmates in a coffee shop to write the plan together. Some students have become so accustomed to such kind of learning behaviour and find it difficult to make adjustments.

Online learning, on the other hand, is mainly delivered through an asynchronous learning mode. This means that your questions posted on the online discussion board may not get answered immediately. You may have to wait several hours or even days before seeing some meaningful replies. Of course, you can use Skype, MSN, and other Internet tools to chat with your virtual classmates and professor. To some students, however, this can be challenging, particularly if they are residing in different time zones around the world.

People from All Walks of Life

One of the issues for students taking online classes is that they are not too willing to accept different opinions or see things from a different perspective. In a traditional university setting, classes are mostly filled with students with similar cultural background, with a relatively small percentage of international students. In online education, however, your classmates may be joining the programme from different continents. Are you willing to work with people from all walks of life? You need to have an open mind when working with a virtual global team. Let me give you a quick example to illustrate this point. In one of my online MBA classes, I had a student, a female Canadian named Susan (not her real name), who felt very uncomfortable after finding out the names and nationalities of her team members.

Her team members included:

Saptarshi – from Pakistan

Katy – from Iran

Muhammad – from the UAE

Trinh – from Vietnam

Susan asked me to help her switch to another team that was made up mainly of North Americans. If you were Susan, would you have felt uncomfortable as well? I asked her to stay in the team because this would allow her to gain some international exposure. Interestingly enough, her team project turned out nicely at the end. In fact, she was working with some of the most brilliant students in my class:

Saptarshi – an agricultural expert in Pakistan

Katy – an IT/Web guru in Iran

Muhammad – the ambassador of an African country, residing in the UAE

Trinh – the managing director of a 5-star hotel in Vietnam

What I'm trying to say is that you need to have an open mind, you must be culturally sensitive, and you have to be willing to see things from a different perspective if you want to be a successful online student.

How This Book Is Organized

This book is written in a serial manner to guide you through the whole university selection process. To find out what graduate business degree programme is best for you, it is important for you to have a clear understanding of your own objectives. Why do you want to pursue such a degree? Is it related to getting a promotion at work? Do you want to learn something new, or just fulfill your self-esteem? Do you want to go for an academically challenging programme, or do you prefer to take an easy ride in your e-learning journey? These questions are important for your university selection, and I will discuss them further in the next chapter.

As we all know, a freshwater fish cannot survive in the sea and a saltwater fish will not feel comfortable in a pond environment. The same can be said about your learning style and the university environment that you are getting into. In chapter 3, I will help you understand your own learning style and then fit that with the right kind of university for your online study.

Once you have a good understanding of your academic needs, you can shop around for the university. There are thousands of online programmes on the web, so choosing one is not a simple task. Before sending in your money for enrollment, why don't you ask the universities a bunch of questions to see how they respond? In chapter 4, I have prepared 40 questions for you to ask, and I hope you can get some meaningful answers from the universities to which you are thinking of applying. Through this Q&A process, I hope you can better evaluate the suitability of your university and programme.

Nowadays, one can find all kinds of aggressive marketing campaigns on the Internet and it may be difficult for you to distinguish the good ones from the bad. That is why I have dedicated chapter 5 to discuss the issue of diploma mills to help you avoid the traps. Subsequently, in chapter 6, I will discuss how you can verify the legitimacy of universities. In your university selection, I think it is more important to choose one that maintains high academic standards and not just one that meets the bare minimum standard. This is where the term "accreditation" comes into the picture. Since it can be a confusing topic, I have dedicated the whole of chapter 7 to it. I hope that, by going through these chapters, you can further narrow down your choice of university and find out the best graduate business programme to pursue.

Since many of my MBA students are interested in pursuing online DBA and PhD, I have dedicated chapter 9 to provide them with additional information about these emerging doctoral degrees for business students. Finally, in the last chapter I will show you some tips for your online study. Are you ready to begin this exciting e-learning journey and get the degree that you have been long dreaming for? Don't stop reading here. Turn your dreams into action!

Chapter 2 - Why a Graduate Business Degree?

The M.B.A. Letters in Your Business Card

My friend Patrick is a Chartered Accountant (CA) and also a Certified Public Accountant (CPA) who has a super busy work schedule. His blackberry keeps blinking every few minutes. Getting him to go out for dinner needs probably three weeks of advanced booking. So I was kind of astonished when he pulled me aside several years ago and said, "Ken, I want to get an MBA degree. Can you show me the quickest and cheapest way to do it?" To help him out, I replied with the following bunch of questions:

- Are you trying to learn new knowledge with your MBA?
- Are you planning to make some new friends to expand your circle of friends?
- Do you intend to get a job promotion after receiving your degree?
- Do you care if the university is a prestigious one?

- Are you willing to invest a good amount of your valuable time to study?
- Are you willing to pay a premium to go for a decent MBA programme?

To my surprise, Patrick answered "No" to all of my questions. So I asked, "What exactly do you want to get out of your MBA degree?" He replied, "The M.B.A. letters to put after my name on my business card, so that my clients can view me more of an accountant who has good business sense instead of just a fast number cruncher."

I ended up recommending that he take an inexpensive online MBA programme from a government-run Australian university. A year and half later, Patrick completed his MBA study. To my understanding, he barely passed his courses and I doubt he made any good friends from the class. But to him, this programme was the best one for him because he was able to get his legitimate MBA degree in just 1.5 years for his purpose: the three letters after his name.

As you can see from this real-life example, what was best for Patrick may not be best for you. Thus, blindly asking people to tell you the best MBA programme is usually fruitless, as one needs to first understand his or her needs for pursing such a degree.

Requirement for Job Promotion

In some multinational firms and government agencies, they have well-published employee promotion guidelines. Having a graduate degree, in most cases, helps you move up the chain to seek a senior position. However, you need to be clear on the precise degree requirement. For example, some organizations require your Master's degree to come from a government-recognized university, while others need your degree or university to be accredited by certain accreditation agencies such as the Association to Advance Collegiate Schools of Business (AACSB), the Association of MBAs (AMBA), the European Foundation for Management Development (EFMD), or one of the six regional accrediting agencies from the United States.

It would be a pity if the MBA degree that you have worked so hard for turns useless simply because it does not meet the stated requirement by your organization. My advice? Check with your human resource experts to clarify the degree requirement, if any.

High-paying Job for Fresh Graduates?

One of the common mistakes that young university students make is believing an MBA degree can always get them the super high salary that they have been dreaming of. As a senior marketer who has been working in the industry, I can tell you that your salary is mainly driven by three major factors: your work experience, education level, and personality. Hence, getting a good degree alone will not get you a six-figure salary in Canada, especially if you are a fresh university graduate who does not have any significant full-time working experience.

Top business schools always promote how high a salary their MBA graduates are making after programme completion. While post-programme salary information is a good indicator, it may not reflect the whole picture. For example, what if the MBA class is made up of students who are already getting great pay prior to entering the programme? Consider, for the instance, two universities:

University A: Students' average salary (before: $80,000; after: $95,000)

University B: Students' average salary (before: $40,000; after: $75,000)

If you ask me to determine which of the two universities is better, I would pick the second one even though their students have a lower average salary after degree completion.

A Stepping Stone for Another Field

A graduate business degree such as an MBA provides a great platform to help students switch fields. This is because in a typical MBA programme, you will gain exposure in all key functional areas, such as finance, marketing, economics, operations, human resources, and information technology. I have seen scientists becoming Venture Capital (VC) associates after earning the degree, while family physicians have become managing directors in pharmaceutical companies afterwards.

The MBA was originally designed as a "generalist" degree to develop managers for organizations, not experts in a particular field. If you are a management consultant and want to be an IT expert, studying for an MBA is the wrong approach because the programme will only touch upon the e-business/IT subject at a strategic level; it will not get into the hard core IT programming details that you are looking for. Even though more and more universities are launching those "specialized" MBAs with concentration in a certain functional area, the depth of knowledge being taught may not be sufficient. Remember, an MBA degree, no matter how it is shaped or modified, is designed to help you to become a better "manager".

If you are trying to be a financial expert, perhaps you should pursue a CFA designation and not an MBA degree. Similarly, if you want to be a technical expert, I would suggest that you enrol in a diploma programme at a local college to sharpen your skills with those Cisco or Microsoft certifications.

Instant Networking Opportunity

Studying for an online degree is a great way to make new friends. My MBA students call it an "instant networking opportunity" because you will be working with your virtual classmates on team projects throughout your study. The question is, where do you want your virtual classmates to come from? This is a key question to consider because each university is good at attracting certain kinds of students to take their online programmes.

Let me give you a real-world example. I teach at U21Global where my MBA students come from over 72 countries. I have a few Canadian students and one of them is very happy. This is because he is in the importing and exporting business; the online programme provides him with the right platform to find business partners in other countries. Whenever he needs to visit a client in Japan, he will notify his classmates in the discussion forum so that they can get together in Tokyo and bring him up to speed about the latest business and political environment in Japan. To him, online education helps him open doors to the world of global business.

On the other hand, I have another Canadian student who keeps complaining about the lack of local students in the programme. She is often the only Canadian in the virtual classroom and hence cannot share much shopping tips for Christmas shopping or chitchat political issues with her classmates. I guess she would feel much better if most of her classmates were coming from Canada, even if they were residing in different provinces across the country. Thus, you need to check out the student profile of your prospective online degree programme prior to enrollment to avoid disappointment.

Chapter 3 - Fitting Your Learning Style with the University's Pedagogy

Six Types of Pedagogy

Pedagogy refers to how education is being delivered to the students. As you can imagine, there are many ways to learn and teach. The best pedagogy, in my opinion, is the one that best fits your own learning style. Over the past several years, I have had the opportunity to teach in various online programmes. I was fortunate to gain exposure to the different kinds of pedagogy used by these online programmes. Is there a perfect one that I can recommend? No. This is simply because each pedagogy has its own advantages and disadvantages. My suggestion is that you ask your prospective universities a lot of questions so that you will understand the pedagogy they are using. If they do not want to tell you the details, there is usually something not good that they want to hide and this will be a red flag in your university selection.

To give you an analogy, there are all kinds of restaurants in a city. Some restaurants serve fast food while others are upscale ones good for fine dining. Is there a perfect type of restaurant? No, as it really depends on your situation and context. Let's say you are in an airport and trying to grab some food prior to boarding the plane; then fine dining is definitely not a good idea because it may take too long. It would be much wiser to get a quick bite at McDonald's or Tim Hortons. On the other hand, if you have lots of time and money is not an issue, then why not enjoy a decent meal in a fine restaurant and spend the night there? What is best for others may not be suitable for you. Coming back to our university selection discussion, you really need to first figure out your preferred learning style, and then find the ideal university that can accommodate your needs. From my experience and observation, there are six major types of pedagogy, namely:

1. Textbook-based programme
2. Discussion Board–based programme
3. Research Paper–based programme
4. Proctored Examination–based programme
5. Facebook-based programme
6. Content-enhanced programme

In the following pages, I will discuss each of these pedagogies in great detail and show you some examples.

Textbook-based Programme

In this kind of programme, you will be reading books all the time. For example, let's say a marketing course spans over 12 weeks, and there are 24 chapters in the textbook. You will probably read the first two chapters in week 1, the next two chapters in week 2, and so on until the whole book is finished. In the online discussion board, every week your professor will probably ask you some questions that are related to the assigned reading. You may also be asked to complete some multiple-choice questions online as well on a weekly basis.

The beauty of such online programme is that as long as you are willing to spend time to do your textbook reading, you should be able to complete your discussion board and paper assignments easily. This is because most of the answers can be found from the textbook. The route to obtaining high marks is straightforward: read the textbook, lift the standard answers from the textbook, and add in your personal or business experience to complete the assignment. Since you will know precisely what chapter you are supposed to read throughout the whole course, you can plan your study schedule ahead and read some chapters in advance for better preparation. As a result, this kind of programme also fits pretty well with those who do not like surprises.

That said, a textbook-based programme is not suitable for everybody. If you do not have the habit of reading books on a regular basis, you may find it very difficult. Don't even think about squeezing time on a Sunday night to read through two chapters because it is very painful. Be honest with yourself. Do you really enjoy reading a thick textbook? Moreover, some students may find this kind of programme a bit boring due to the lack of interaction with other students. An example of such programme can be found in universities such as American Sentinel University in the United States. Learn more at http://www.americansentinel.edu.

Discussion Board–based Programme

If you are not a book lover, you may want to consider programmes that utilize a different pedagogy. For example, some programmes have a strong focus on discussion board activities and you are required to be present in the discussion forums at least three or four times a week. You are also supposed to post comprehensive analysis with proper citing and referencing, and not just short postings of the "I agree with your comments" type. Your grade will be affected by many factors, such as the timing of your post, its length and writing style, and the depth of your analysis. Very often, the professor will be asking open-ended questions that may not have a standard or correct answer. It is all about your arguments and justifications. Hence, you are not only required to share your unique insights, but also to critique several of your classmates' postings properly each week.

While a textbook may still be used in the course, you may not be required to read through all of the chapters. This kind of programme is great for those who do not like to read textbooks. In addition to writing team papers, you are supposed to play an active role in the discussion board with your team members and the class. This kind of programme fits very well with those who like to speak up in the class and argue with their online classmates.

Since it may be difficult to achieve an "A" due to lack of certainty and predictability, this kind of programme may not be ideal for some students. Moreover, those students who do not like to mingle with their online classmates on a regular basis may find it challenging. An example of such programme can be found at U21Global Graduate School. Learn more at http://www.u21global.edu.sg.

Research Paper–based Programme

In this type of programme, research plays a key role in your study. While you have to complete some online discussion forum work and write a few weekly short papers, the main focus is on your research paper. At the beginning of the course, you will consult with the professor to finalize your research topic, then you have to gradually complete this lengthy research paper week by week and show your professor some drafts throughout the course. Based on the feedback that you receive from the professor, and your Internet findings, you keep polishing the research paper until it is ready for submission at the end of the course.

This kind of programme is suitable for those who like to do research. You are often given the freedom to choose your research topic so it can be really interesting and relevant, particularly to those small business owners who want to find ways to improve upon their business operations. Students who like to write also appreciate the regular feedback from the professor on their paper assignments. Furthermore, a textbook may not be required so as long as you have access to the Internet. You can complete the programme anywhere on this planet, without worrying about the need to carry around the heavy textbooks.

However, a research paper–based programme can be viewed by some as boring. You may be working alone most of the time especially when the discussion forum plays a minimum role, if any, in your study. An example of such programme can be found in Trident University International. Learn more at http://www.tuiu.edu.

Proctored Examination–based Programme

Another type of graduate degree programme that can be taken remotely is based on proctored examination. That is, your success is determined by your ability to pass examinations that you take in person at a nearby proctored examination centre. This kind of programme usually has a relatively easy entrance requirement. You join the programme, sign up for a course, receive the course materials via snail mail, and then take your proctored examination whenever you feel ready. Although you may get accepted easily into such programme, passing the examination can be rather difficult.

Unlike other types of programmes in which continuous assessment is used, you are assessed solely by how well or poorly you do in the proctored examination. This type of programme is good for those who have no problem memorizing textbook materials and writing long examination papers for several hours. Such programme is great for those who prefer to study alone, without worrying about the free-riders in team projects, or the need to log into the learning management system (LMS) several times a week to make the weekly postings.

However, the lack of regular interaction with your classmates may lead you to find this mode of study boring. Furthermore, many of these programmes are paper-based, meaning there is no video to watch, no interactive online content to view, and no wiki or blogs to play with during the programme. Some universities try to offset these disadvantages by setting up an online portal for the students to share ideas and thoughts. However, since most of these portals are not course specific, you may find it challenging to get specific help for the particular course that you are taking at the time you need such help. Examples of such programme can be found in the Online MBA programme from Edinburgh Business School of Heriot-Watt University in the UK. Learn more at http://www.ebsglobal.net.

Facebook–based Programme

One of the most interesting developments in online education is the use of the social networking platform for course delivery. In 2010, the first Facebook-based online MBA programme was launched. It allows potential students to view all of the course materials such as lecture video, case studies, and course notes using a Facebook application over its platform, prior to enrolling into the programme. Similar to the programme based on proctored examination, you are only required to take the final examination when you are ready to pay and sit for the examination. An example of this kind of programme can be found at London School of Business and Finance in the UK. Learn more at: http://apps.facebook.com/lsbfglobalmba.

Content-enhanced Programme

By now, you should have acquired some ideas about the various kinds of online programmes out there. However, what if you prefer a programme that utilizes a bit of everything? Well, the good news is that such kind of programme exists and I will simply call it the content-enhanced programme. In this kind of learning environment, you will come across short video clips, discussion forums, blogs, wikis, and online multiple-choice questions, and you can view some course materials directly on the LMS.

This kind of programme will certainly attract those students who are tech-savvy. They will appreciate the rich web content and the wide variety of online activities throughout their study. This also means, however, that you must be willing to learn about new technology and use these advanced web tools comfortably on a regular basis. Otherwise, you will have a tough time catching up in class. An example of a content-enhanced programme can be found at Southern New Hampshire University in the United States. Learn more at http://www.snhu.edu.

Learning Management System

How about the LMS that is used to deliver the course content? Does it affect the programme's pedagogy? Well, I think you should not be too concerned about the kind of LMS that the university is currently using. It is quite true that during the 1990s, there was a big gap in LMS quality because there was a wide range of vendors providing such e-learning solutions. However, after a decade of vendor consolidation and feature improvement, all major LMS serve similar functions with pretty acceptable user interface in my opinion. Hence, you should not really care whether your university is using a commercial LMS (e.g., Blackboard, WebCT, Desire2Learn, and First Class), open-source LMS (e.g., Moodle), or even a proprietary one (e.g., CourseNet).

Chapter 4 – 40 Essential Questions To Ask Your School

Knowing More about the Programme

A common mistake that students make in applying to graduate school is not asking enough questions prior to enrollment. Once you have sent in your money, it may cost you time, money, and lots of frustration to withdraw from a programme. No matter how great a university or its programme may sound, there is still a possibility that it may not meet your needs and expectations. Even if you are confident that the university you are dreaming for is perfect for you, go through this chapter to ensure you do not miss out any key areas for checking. Enrolling in a Master's degree programme is a serious matter, so do not take it lightly. After all, you are making a long-term academic commitment. In this chapter, I am going to present you with a wide range of questions that you should ask. These questions also point you to the appropriate chapters of this book for further reading.

Degree-Granting Authority

Question 1: Is the university recognized by the Canadian government?

In other words, does the university you are trying to get into have any official degree-granting authority? Believe it or not, there are many fake universities or low-tier education providers that claim to have degree-granting power but in fact do not. As a result, you have to watch out for the so-called "diploma mills". Read chapter 5 to learn more about these diploma mill scams and then continue with chapter 6 to learn about the ways to confirm the legal status of a Canadian university.

Question 2: What if the university is located outside of Canada? How do I know if the foreign government recognizes it?

In each country, there should be some kind of ministry or department that governs the degree-granting power of universities. Very often, an official university list is published on their respective web sites. Later in chapter 6, I will show you how to check the legal status of a foreign university in the United States, the United Kingdom, and Australia.

Question 3: Who awards the qualifications?

This is a really important question to ask. You may be taking a programme at University "A" and paying tuition fees to it throughout your study, but that does not automatically mean the degree you will earn will come from that university. While it may sound like a stupid question to ask, you have to be 100% certain about which institution of higher education is granting you the degree, no matter what university crests and names appear on your testamur (certificate). This can be a confusing issue because there are many joint programmes out there, plus some British universities (e.g., University of Wales) allow other colleges and schools to offer degree programmes on their behalf via the British accreditation process.

Reputation of the University

Question 4: Has the university achieved any kind of accreditation?

I have dedicated the whole of chapter 7 to the topic of accreditation because it means different things in different countries. In a nutshell, you want to find out if the university to which you are trying to apply has not only met the minimum required standard, but has also achieved some kind of "quality seal" from the government or third party accrediting agencies.

Question 5: How is the university being ranked?

Watch out! There are lots of fake university rankings appearing on the web that are being put up by the universities' direct marketers or affiliates. To get a rough idea of a university's relative position in the education market, you should check the university ranking as published by the major newspaper and weekly magazine of the country where the university is headquartered. You can also refer to those global university rankings as provided by QS/TopMBA, *Bloomberg Businessweek* magazine, and the UK's *Financial Times* newspaper. See chapter 7 for details.

Question 6: Does it run any executive education programme for corporate clients?

Another way to learn about the quality of a university's business programme is to check if it is currently providing any executive training programme (i.e., non-degree programme) to major corporations or government agencies. As you can imagine, these "corporate clients" would have done their due diligence prior to sending their managers to attend these expensive short-term training courses. While this may not be a scientific measure of a university's reputation and programme quality, it is a lazy person's way to piggyback on others' research.

Quality of the Programme

Question 7: Who are the professors?

The GIGO (garbage in, garbage out) principle applies to the education sector. If the professor is not highly qualified, you cannot expect too much from your programme. The rule of the game is very simple: Good professors teach at good schools in general. Of course, there are exceptions, particularly if the professor is a young person who needs to accumulate teaching hours (just like pilots), or when the job market is very bad during his or her year of graduation. Check the name of the university that they graduated from. Do their terminal degrees come from AACSB-, AMBA-, or EFMD-accredited universities? If not, are they government-run institutions?

Question 8: Do they hold PhD or DBA degrees?

Believe it or not, not all professors hold a terminal degree. The best schools should have all of their professors (irrespective of their rank) holding a terminal degree. In reality, this percentage may drop to 90% to 95% for some pretty good universities while the tier-2 institutions may only have half of their faculty members holding PhD or DBA degrees. Perhaps you may be thinking that a good teacher does not necessarily have to have earned such terminal degree. Yes, that can be true, but do not forget that you may want to pursue further graduate study after completing your MBA degree. In that case, you would need a mentor to guide you on your research activities and only a PhD or DBA degree holder would have gained sufficient research experience to give you meaningful advice.

Question 9: Where are the professors located?

Since online education allows students from different countries to study, your university may also be hiring faculty members from overseas. In my opinion, the best learning experience can be achieved if your professors have an international background. Think about it. How can you properly learn about the emerging economy in India, China, or Vietnam if your International Business course professor has never travelled to Asia? It is possible, but highly unlikely. If you are interested in learning about "Islamic Finance", which is a specialized field in finance, you should probably look for a professor who has lived or worked in the Middle East, and not just someone who has studied this subject in the library.

Question 10: Do they have industry experience?

If you just want to learn about some academic theories, the professor's background is not too important as long as he or she can teach properly. In your Master-level study, however, you may want to think out of the box and challenge the applicability of academic theories in real-life business situations. In this case, you need to have a professor who has actually worked in the field for some time. Hence, you should look for professors who have gained some industry experience, regardless of whether they have worked in the industry themselves or have acted as consultants for major corporate clients. Check the professor's biography or CV as posted on the university's web site.

Question 11: Can you show me the typical student profile?

In addition to learning from the professors, students at a Master-level programme also learn a great deal from their classmates because they will be involved in lots of team assignments. If most of your MBA classmates are fresh graduates who have limited working experience, I guess the scope of the class discussion would be very limited. However, if most of your classmates are senior executives who have a wide range of work experience in different industries, you could probably gain quite a bit of industry insights from them. Things that you can check include the students' age groups, industry, nationality, and gender.

Tuition Fee Matters

Question 12: Can I pay my tuition fee online?

You may think it is a no-brainer, but the fact is that not all universities are technology-savvy, especially when it comes to financial matters. As you may have read from the news, some universities only accept payment in the form of a certified cheque, or via bank wires. Even if your university accepts payments via credit cards online, many of them only accept VISA or MasterCard. If you are using an American Express card or those niche cards like JCB, Discovery, UnionPay, or Diners Club card, please double-check with your university to avoid last minute panic! How about PayPal credits? Well, I do not think universities accept PayPal yet, but that may change in the future.

Question 13: How much is the tuition fee if I pay it all at once?

Yes, you may indeed get a discount if you pay your tuition in full. Some universities even give you a further discount if you sign up for the programme early on in the year! Check with your university and do not make assumptions about the fees until you get a black-and-white confirmation in e-mail, fax, or letter.

Question 14: Do you have any installment plan? If Yes, what does the installment payment schedule look like?

Paying thirty or more thousand dollars upfront may be a big financial challenge for most people. As such, some universities allow students to pay their tuition fees in installments. Please note, however, that you have to pay some interest if you follow the installment plans. In other words, the total sum you will be paying using the installment plan will be higher than what you would pay if you pay your fees upfront in a single lump sum. The gap varies a lot. Even though the interest rate is very low around the world in 2011, the premium you will be paying via installment may be up to 10% in some cases. Double-check with your university to avoid surprises. Again, get them to confirm your tuition fee in black and white.

Question 15: Can I withdraw from a course and get a refund? If Yes, what are the conditions?

It depends. Some universities allow you to "test" the first course of a programme while others do not provide any refund at all once you have started the programme. If you have good reasons for withdrawal (e.g., personal health issues, special work assignment), you may be given a partial refund as long as you withdraw from the course during the first week or two. Different universities have different policies on this matter, so do not make any assumption.

Question 16: Is my tuition fee tax-deductible?

For Canadians, you know our lovely Canada Revenue Agency (CRA) has all kinds of tax credit schemes, and they evolve from time to time. Surprisingly, many Canadians do not know that they may be eligible for tax refund on their tuition fee paid for their online study. To accomplish this, you need to first download the required Revenue Canada forms (T2202E and TL11D) from Revenue Canada's web site:

http://www.cra-arc.gc.ca/E/pub/tp/it516r2/it516r2-e.html#P71_6821

Then, identify yourself as a full-time or part-time student on the form and complete your program details there. Once the form is completed, e-mail or fax it to your university's registrar to have it stamped, signed, and dated. Ask the university to send you back the completed form, which you can then attach to your personal tax filing to receive the tax credits, if any. Please note that not all universities are eligible. You have to confirm your eligibility with the local Revenue Canada tax services office. They are required by law to maintain a current list of institutions outside of Canada that are recognized as universities for this tax-credit purpose. If the officer is confused, ask him or her to read paragraph 118.5(1)(b) of the Federal Act.

Question 17: Do you have any entrance scholarship or bursary?

Some universities run their online programmes as a money-making venture. Many of the principles in sales management apply. For example, depending on the timing of your application, you may be able to seek some discounts if the university or its agents are eager to sign you up as a student (i.e., close the deal!). Hence, it will not hurt to ask during your "negotiation" with the university if you are qualified for any kind of tuition fee discounts, in the name of an entrance scholarship or bursary. Your chance of getting a break on tuition fee will be higher if your score in the Graduate Management Admission Test (GMAT) is high, or if you have some unique work experience that you can bring to the table to enhance the quality of the class.

Other Money Matters

Question 18: Do I have to pay for the examination?

Don't laugh; some universities have hidden fees like this. They may call it an examination sitting fee, or an assignment-grading fee. In the unlikely event that you failed a course, you may be allowed to take a supplementary examination later, but of course, there is a fee for this service.

Question 19: Do I have to pay to receive my testamur?

If you do not reside in the same city as the university you are applying to, and you cannot attend the graduation ceremony to collect your testamur (certificate) in person, you may need to pay some fees to have your testamur mailed to you via courier service. Even if you are willing to travel to another country to attend the graduation ceremony, there may still be some fees (e.g., membership fee for alumni association, or gown rental) that you have to pay right there at the venue.

Question 20: Do I have to pay for my student card?

Not all universities will issue a physical student card to an online student. In some cases, the student card is available on request and there may be a small fee to cover the handling and mailing. With this student card, you "may" be able to gain access to local university libraries or enjoy student discounts on buses and trains. Isn't it good to be a student again?

Admission Matters

Question 21: Do I need to take the GMAT?

The GMAT has traditionally been used as an indicator to evaluate the performance of MBA applicants. More and more universities, however, are moving away from such requirement, while some give little weights to the GMAT as part of the overall evaluation process. If you have substantial working experience, the GMAT requirement may even be waived. As such, you are urged to check this requirement with your university.

Question 22: Do I need to take the TOEFL?

If your undergraduate study was completed at an English-speaking university, you should not be required to take the TOEFL examination. That said, some tier-1 universities may still want to see your TOEFL score if your undergraduate degree comes from certain developing countries. Hence, it won't hurt to ask your university for clarification.

Question 23: Do I need to maintain a certain CGPA in order to apply?

It really depends. Even if your university has clearly stated a minimum requirement for your cumulative grade point average (CGPA) in your undergraduate study, this policy may not be enforced 100% of the time, especially if you have unique quality or experience that you can bring to the MBA class.

Question 24: I don't have any full-time working experience. Can I still apply?

In general, MBA applicants should have already acquired at least two or three years of full-time working experience. However, fresh graduates who have good extra-curricular activities (e.g., being the president or executive committee member of a student organization) may be considered for enrolment into an MBA programme.

Textbook Matters

Question 25: Do I need to buy textbooks separately?

This is a good question to ask. Some universities include the cost of textbook in the tuition fee while others do not. Even if textbooks are provided, you should clarify with the university to see if the shipping fee is also included. In some cases, only the standard "snail mail" postal service is included and students have to pay extra if they want to get the books via courier service such as FedEx or UPS.

Question 26: Where can I source the textbooks?

If the university does not provide textbooks to you directly, you may run into the problem of sourcing them here in Canada. This is particularly the case if the university you are applying to is based in Europe, as those European textbooks may not be available in your local university bookstores. Even if you can order them online at Amazon or Chapters/Indigo, the shipping time may be two to three weeks instead of days because they have to source the books for you from the European book distributors. Another issue is the textbook edition. Even if you can source the textbooks in Canada, they may be the "North American edition" instead of the "International English edition" that your school is using. The chapters may be shuffled around and the chapter-end questions may be slightly different in some cases.

Question 27: Is there any e-book version of the textbook that I can use?

Some universities have carefully designed their curriculum and use textbooks that have an e-book edition. This comes in handy as you can just access the e-book instead of carrying the heavy textbook around in the office or at home. In some cases, the e-books may be provided to the students either free of charge or at a large institutional discount. Hence, you should check with the university to see how these e-books should be sourced. When I say e-books, I refer to either a PDF file or one that requires a sealer such as the Adobe Digital Edition. Some e-books have a digital right management (DRM) restriction that prevents you from distributing them elsewhere, or from making printed copies. A major provider of these online textbooks is CourseSmart; you can learn more at http://www.coursesmart.com.

Student Support Matters

Question 28: Is there a local student chapter that I can join?

Many online MBA programmes are able to attract students from different continents. It would be good if you could meet other online students locally for social networking or even homework assistance. Some universities have local student chapters in different countries to bring their current students together. You should check with your university to see if these student groups are available locally.

Question 29: Is there an alumni association that I can join after graduation?

It may sound weird to talk about an alumni association when you have not yet enrolled in such an online programme. However, don't forget that pursuing an MBA is a great investment. If you can join a university that maintains a strong alumni association, why not? It may open some doors for you later, both professionally and academically.

Question 30: Does your IT support team operate 24/7/365?

To be honest with you, I have never come across an online student who has not yet come across any kind of IT issues during his or her study. It may be a minor password log-in issue during the orientation, or a severe paper uploading problem during the final examination. No matter what kind of technical problem it is, you will need help from the IT experts for sure. If you do not reside in the same time zone as your university, then an IT support team that operates around the clock will be essential.

Question 31: What kind of online library access do I have?

Virtually all universities give you access to their online journals, magazines, e-books, and all types of databases. However, the scope of subscription may vary a lot. At bare minimum, your e-library should allow you to access databases such as ProQuest and ScienceDirect. If it has subscriptions to InfoSci Journals and Emerald Management First then it is even better. To do a reality check, ask the university if students can easily access top journals such as *Journal of Marketing, Journal of Marketing Research*, and *Marketing Letters*.

Study Matters

Question 32: What is the length of the programme?

Be careful when checking the length (duration) of the programme. Some universities may mislead you by saying the whole programme can be done in just a year or two, without stating clearly that it is assuming you are doing it on a full-time basis. However, most students who pursue an online MBA are working professionals who still want to maintain their day job, so you have to check carefully how long such programme will last and what the coursework requirements are. Instead of asking about the programme length, perhaps it is better to ask about the number of courses required to graduate and when these courses are offered throughout the year.

Question 33: How many subjects can I take at the same time?

To prevent high dropout rates, some universities have restrictions on how many subjects (courses) you can take at any particular timeframe. In general, students should be able to do two courses at a time, assuming they also maintain their regular day job. Check with your university about such policy because you may not be able to take three or four courses at a time even if you are a fast learner.

Question 34: How much time should I set aside for study per week?

I think it is a fair question to ask. Frankly speaking, I have come across different kinds of online MBA programmes that have very different workload requirements. In some programmes you may have to log into the LMS once or twice a week to check out the web contents, while in others you may have to log in almost everyday to make lengthy online postings. Never assume that you can make up the time during weekends because in most cases you simply cannot.

Question 35: Is it a self-paced programme?

Yes, some online MBA programmes are self-paced. This means you may be able to submit homework as soon as you are ready, or you can wait until the last week of the course to send in your papers. The beauty of a self-paced programme is that you can control the study schedule. This also implies, however, that other students may not show up in the discussion forums on time as they are also studying on their own schedule. This may create a negative learning environment as students are not studying on the same pace. For example, your question may not get answered by others until weeks later. Thus, it is important to find out if your online MBA programme is a self-paced one.

Question 36: Can I take breaks during the programme?

The fact is that you may want to take a temporary break during your study. Perhaps you want to take a few months off to travel, or you simply need to work on an important company project as assigned by your boss. No matter what your reasons are, it is important that your university is flexible enough to accommodate your needs. Some universities only allow you to take one or two breaks during the programme so you have to find out these restrictions before enrollment. Furthermore, there may be a limitation on the length of the break that you can take.

Question 37: How will I be assessed?

Is there any peer assessment? Will my paper be checked using anti-plagiarism software like turnitin.com? How often do I need to post my messages in the discussion forums? Will I get penalized if my English is not top-notch? Does it matter how often and how long I log into the LMS throughout the week? These are the questions you should ask.

Question 38: If I cannot complete the Master's degree programme, can I get some kind of postgraduate diploma or certificate?

Yes, some universities would give those students who have completed two thirds of their Master-level study a postgraduate diploma or certificate. The fact is that not all MBA students can complete the programme fully for a wide variety of reasons such as financial, workload, and family issues. If this kind of arrangement is available, at least you can get some recognition for the part of study you have completed.

Question 39: Can I transfer my credits from another university?

This is an important question to ask as you may be able to study and pay less with your MBA programme. This is particularly true if you have already completed similar Master-level courses at another institution of higher education.

Question 40: Can I transfer my credits to another university?

Well, this question can be tricky, but it is still an important one. Perhaps you may rephrase it to say, "Do you know if any of your students have problems using their credits to pursue a doctoral degree at another university?"

Chapter 5 - The Diploma Mill Scam

What are Diploma Mills?

In simple terms, diploma mills are fake universities. Any testamur or transcript issued by a diploma mill is just a piece of worthless paper. A fake degree certainly will not open doors for you in the corporate world. Even if you were able to fool the hiring manager with your bogus degree to get a job or promotion, it would not take long for your colleagues or the HR experts to find that out later. In some extreme cases, diploma mill degree holders not only lose their job after being caught, but also get sued by other parties for damages. So, why take the risk of getting yourself into trouble?

Although some students intended to take the shortcut by getting their degrees from diploma mills, others might have applied to diploma mills unintentionally simply because they are not educated about these crooks. Hence, this chapter is written to help you avoid them.

Characteristics of Diploma Mills

The Internet is filled with advertisements from diploma mills around the world. The basic rule is that if it sounds too good to be true, it usually is! Never judge the validity of a university by simply looking at how its web site is designed, as a diploma mill may hire professional graphics designers to do the web design. Similarly, never believe everything you read on the web about a particular university. Diploma mills are known for hiring people to write good reviews for them in blogs, discussion forums, and other web channels. If somebody says "University A is a great one" or "This MBA is the best" in a discussion forum, do not take it at face value even if it is being posted in well-established forums like degreeinfo.com. You simply do not know who these people are. Some sophisticated operators have even developed fake university ranking sites to promote their diploma mills to fool the uneducated.

So, is there any way to identify these troublemakers? The answer is "Yes!" In the following pages, I am going to show you some of the typical characteristics of a diploma mill. If the university to which you are applying demonstrates some or all of these characteristics, you are strongly urged to double-check that university's legality before it gets too late.

1. Detailed information about faculty members is not shown on the web site

Real professors, no matter what rank they currently have (e.g., lecturer, adjunct, assistant, associate, or full professor), always maintain a detailed profile on the university's web site. It should include the professor's research interest, prior work history, and list of publications. Hence, the lack of such detailed information is a good indication of a diploma mill.

2. Lack of physical address

All legitimate universities have proper physical addresses. If the university's "Contact Us" page shows only e-mail addresses and some phone numbers (especially those 1-800 or 1-866 ones) as contact information, there is a high probability that such university is a fake one.

3. Suspicious physical address

What is the likelihood of a legitimate university being located in the same building as a mail-forwarding service centre such as Mail Boxes ETC, FedEx Office, or UPS Store? Very low! A quick Google search on the university's address should provide some insights into this matter. There is a feature on Google Map (maps.google.com) in which you can actually see the street view of the building that you are trying to find. Just drag the yellow human icon on top of the red "A" pin on the map and you will be able to see it. Check it out!

4. Outdated web site

A real university always maintains an up-to-date web site, showing the latest information about its students, faculty, alumni, and upcoming courses or programmes being offered. If the web site is a static one that has not been updated for a while, the chance that such university is a diploma mill would be high.

5. Life experience for credit

Many diploma mills advertise on their sites that you can use your life experience to get credits. The fact is that real universities rarely do that, and even if they do, you are usually required to visit a local authorized exam centre to take a CLEP test. Hence, if a university simply asks you to send in your resume for assessment, it is probably not a serious university that you should consider.

6. Lifetime credential verification service

This function is done by the university's registrar's office, and no legitimate university would ever need to promote it. At least I have never seen one doing so thus far.

7. No need to study, attend class, or take exams

Do you think your family physician can get his or her medical degree without studying, attending classes, or taking exams? I have yet to find any legitimate university that allows people to seek a Master-level degree without studying or writing a thesis or dissertation. If the university allows you to submit just a short, 10-page assignment and use that to get a degree, it is probably not a real university.

8. Get a degree in 7 days!

This is just impossible with a real university, even in 30, 60, or 90 days. Wake up! The shortest MBA is about 9 months of full-time study, while the majority would need 12 to 24 months for programme completion, depending on the country.

9. Order delivery by FedEx or DHL

Does it sound like online shopping? Real universities only issue testamur after a graduation ceremony that takes place once or twice a year. Hence, there is no need for a real university to focus on the delivery mode of their transcript or testamur with such urgency.

10. Exclusive 100% money-back guarantee

Every time I see this on a diploma mill site, I simply cannot stop laughing.

11. Lack of accreditation or government recognition

A diploma mill will never be able to achieve any accreditation status with any legitimate accrediting agency. Thus, the lack of such accreditation status is a good indication that it "may" be a diploma mill.

12. Member of a fake accreditation agency

To address the issue of accreditation, some smart diploma mills simply create fake accreditation agencies to give accreditation themselves. Hence, if your university is a member of any fake accreditation agency, it is a diploma mill for sure.

The Infamous Diploma Mill Lists

There are hundreds of diploma mills around the world. Spotting them may be difficult for the uninformed students but not to the government officials who work for the education department or ministry. In the United States, several states such as Oregon, Maine, and Michigan are well known for their strict policy on education, and the Office of Degree Authorization (ODA) in each of these states maintains an up-to-date list that covers diploma mills operating around the world. These diploma mill lists are available to the public on the ODA web sites. It is a good idea to make good use of these lists to check if the university you are applying to is a diploma mill.

The Oregon List

In the USA, The Oregon Student Assistance Commission Office of Degree Authorization maintains a list of "Unaccredited colleges" on its web site. You can access it at:

http://www.osac.state.or.us/oda/unaccredited.aspx

The Maine List

The Maine Higher Education maintains a "list of Non-Accredited Post-Secondary Universities" list on its web site. You can view it at:

http://www.maine.gov/education/highered/Non-Accredited/non-accredited.htm#DL

The Michigan List

The State of Michigan publishes a document titled "Colleges and Universities Not Accredited by CHEA". You can access it at:

http://www.michigan.gov/documents/Non-accreditedSchools_78090_7.pdf

If you get a "404 error" when accessing this page, just search "Michigan unaccredited university list" in your search engine.

Chapter 6 - List of Legitimate Universities

Is Your University Recognized by the Canadian Government?

The previous chapter discussed the issue of diploma mills. You should avoid these problematic universities during your programme search. It is important to bear in mind, however, that even if the university you are planning to apply is not a diploma mill, it can still be a bad one that has little, if any, recognition in Canada. Hence, you need to ascertain that the degree you are going to seek is one that can be officially used across this country.

In Canada, each provincial government is responsible for evaluating universities headquartered in the province and granting them authority to confer degrees. In general, Canadian degrees are portable across the country so a UBC degree from British Columbia will be recognized in Ontario, while a UofT degree from Ontario will have no problem getting recognition in British Columbia. Please note that there is no federal government agency that governs the issuing of Canadian degrees because it is done at the provincial level.

The CICIC Directory

The easiest way to find out if the Canadian university that you are planning to apply is recognized by the Canadian government is to make use of the Canadian Information Centre for International Credentials (CICIC) Directory. The CICIC, a unit of the Council of Ministers of Education in Canada, maintains an online national database of all recognized colleges and universities in Canada. It is open to the public and there is no service charge. You can access it at:

http://www.cicic.ca/664/directory-of-universities-colleges-and-universities-in-canada.canada

If the link is broken, just visit the cicic.ca web site and find the directory there. All you need to do is to type in the name of the university, and select the type of institution. Since virtually all of the graduate degree programmes in Canada are run by universities, you should select "Public and Private Recognized and Authorized Postsecondary Institutions" during your search.

Departments of Education Across Canada

In addition to the CICIC Directory, you can also check the lists of universities published by provincial governments across Canada. Please note that many of these lists show public universities on the main page. If your chosen university is a private one (less than 5% in Canada), it may be listed under a separate page within the same web site. Private universities are granted the right to issue degrees by the provincial government through its own "Degree Granting Act". Instead of showing you all of the universities in Canada, I am going to list the web sites from which you can find the most updated list of colleges and universities that are approved by the corresponding province. As of this writing, there is no graduate business programme offered by post-secondary institutions in Yukon, Northwest Territories and Nunavut.

British Columbia

Ministry of Advanced Education and Labour Market Development:

http://www.aved.gov.bc.ca/degree-authorization/applicants.htm

Alberta

Ministry of Alberta Advanced Education and Technology:

http://www.advancededucation.gov.ab.ca/post-secondary/institutions/public.aspx

Saskatchewan

Ministry of Advanced Education, Employment and Immigration:

http://www.aeel.gov.sk.ca/post-secondary-educ-Institutions

Manitoba

Ministry of Manitoba Advanced Education and Literacy:

http://www.edu.gov.mb.ca/ael/unicoll/universities.html

Ontario

Ministry of Training, Colleges and Universities:

http://www.tcu.gov.on.ca/eng/postsecondary/schoolsprograms/
university/index.html

Quebec

Ministère de l'Éducation:

http://www.mels.gouv.qc.ca/sections/demandeAdmission/index.
asp?page=universitaire

New Brunswick

Department of Post-Secondary Education, Training and Labour:

http://www.gnb.ca/0105/ps/univ_ccnb-e.asp

Prince Edward Island

Department of Education and Early Childhood Development:

http://www.gov.pe.ca/infopei/index.php3?number=787&lang=E

Nova Scotia

Department of Education:

http://www.ednet.ns.ca/contact/universities.shtml

Newfoundland and Labrador

Department of Education:

http://www.ed.gov.nl.ca/edu/postsecondary/public.html

Yukon

Advanced Education branch of the Department of Education:

http://www.education.gov.yk.ca/advanceded/

Northwest Territories

Ministry of Education, Culture and Employment:

http://www.ece.gov.nt.ca/

Nunavut

Department of Education:

http://www.edu.gov.nu.ca/apps/authoring/dspPage.
aspx?page=home

Is Your University Recognized by the American Government?

Without doubt, the educational system in the United States is way more complicated than that in Canada. There are lots of diploma mills, unaccredited universities, and accredited ones. If you are planning to pursue a degree from a university that is based in the USA, it is important for you to check the university's status to ascertain that it is recognized by the American government.

The USDOE and CHEA Accreditation Databases

Although the U.S. Department of Education (USDOE) does not accredit universities directly, it is required by law to maintain an online database called "The Database of Accredited Postsecondary Institutions and Programs". It is open to the public and there is no charge for the service. When your chosen university is listed in this database, it means that it is a legitimate one that is recognized by the American Government. It will also show the kind of accreditation that the university is currently holding:

http://ope.ed.gov/accreditation/Search.aspx

The same database is mirrored by the Council for Higher Education Accreditation (CHEA):

http://www.chea.org/search/default.asp

Please note that the above database does not indicate the quality of the university or its programmes; you can find top universities like Harvard University and also bottom ones that barely meet the minimum standard as required by the USDOE. To find out which university is a "good" one, you will need to read the next chapter on "Accreditation" because there are different kinds of accreditation in the United States.

Unaccredited Universities vs. Diploma Mills in the USA

How about those universities that have not sought any kind of accreditation? Is it true that unaccredited American universities are equal to diploma mills? Does it mean that all unaccredited universities are bad ones that I should avoid? Since this is a confusing topic, let me spend a minute or two to talk about it.

Diploma mills, as I have mentioned in Chapter 5, are just fake universities that issue worthless papers and degrees. Thus, never apply to a diploma mill under any circumstances. In terms of accreditation, one thing you should bear in mind is that institutional accreditation does not exist in Canada. Hence, the lack of accreditation is not a problem for Canadian universities and their programmes at all.

However, the situation is very different in the United States. Not all legitimate American universities have sought accreditation from either national, regional, or management-specific accreditation agencies. Holding a degree from an "unaccredited-yet-legitimate" American university may or may not be problematic depending on where you are residing. This is because not all U.S. states accept unaccredited degrees. Hence, an unaccredited degree may be legally used in one state for study and job purposes, but this same degree may be viewed as an illegal one in another American state. As a result, an unaccredited degree may be treated the same way as a degree coming from a diploma mill in certain U.S. states.

The general rule of thumb is that your American degree should come from an "accredited" university if you intend to apply for a U.S. government job. Hence, unless you are going to stay in a particular state forever, you should not waste time and money to study at an unaccredited university because you may want to work elsewhere later. The best degree should be one that is highly portable and has no acceptance issue not only across the United States, but also in other parts of the world.

Is Your University Recognized by the British Government?

The United Kingdom is one of the countries that have been pioneering the concept of distance education, so it is not uncommon for Canadians to pursue online degrees from British universities. However, just like the situation in the United States, there are good ones and bad ones out there in the United Kingdom. There are about 157 higher education institutions in the UK that have degree-granting authority, as empowered by a Royal Charter, an Act of Parliament, or the Privy Council. Therefore, before sending in your money to enroll at a British university, you are strongly urged to check the university's legal status with the corresponding British government agency. A list of recognized UK universities can be viewed online at the web site of the Department for Business Innovation & Skills (BIS):

http://www.dcsf.gov.uk/recognisedukdegrees/index.
cfm?fuseaction=institutes.list&InstituteCategoryID=1&OrderBy
=Category

In the United Kingdom, some colleges offer courses or programmes that may lead to a degree awarded by one of the above UK universities. These colleges are known as the "Listed Bodies". You can look them up from the following BIS site:

http://www.dcsf.gov.uk/recognisedukdegrees/index. cfm?fuseaction=institutes.list&InstituteCategoryID=2&OrderBy =Category

Please note that the BIS does not rank universities. Please read the next chapter to see how "good" British universities can be found.

Is Your University Recognized by the Australian Government?

In Australia, the Department of Education, Employment and Workplace Relations maintains an online list of higher education providers. It can be accessed at:

http://www.goingtouni.gov.au/Main/CoursesAndProviders/ ProvidersAndCourses/HigherEducationProviders/Default.htm

As a student, you should view the above list of universities as those that meet the minimum standard as required by the Australian government. No ranking is given to these colleges and universities.

Chapter 7 - All About Accreditation

Importance of Accreditation

So, what exactly is accreditation? In layman's terms, accreditation is the "Seal of Approval" in education. An analogy is the ISO9001 certification given to a manufacturing plant. Depending on the type of accreditation that is being sought, accreditation may be applied to the whole university or to just a particular programme.

Accrediting agencies are those third parties, non-profit organizations that issue accreditation status to universities. As part of the accreditation process, these agencies usually send well-respected professors as inspectors to check the universities every few years. The inspectors spend time to interview the faculty members, talk to the students, go over the operation with the university administrators, and then conduct a thorough assessment of the university's curriculum. They may even look at how faculty members are recruited and trained. Since the evaluation process covers many areas, the time it takes a university to get accredited varies, ranging from a year up to five or six years. Some accreditations such as U.S. Regional Accreditation (RA) and AACSB are relatively more difficult to get because they have more stringent requirements than others.

Although accreditation is a voluntary process that can be time consuming and expensive, most reputable universities have sought accreditation to demonstrate their programme quality to the public. Please note that once an accreditation is granted, it will not last forever. A university has to apply for re-accreditation with the accreditation agency every few years. Some universities receive a one-year accreditation while others may have a longer one (e.g., three or five years).

Triple Crown - World's Top Accreditations for Business Universities

The discussion on accreditation can be tricky, particularly when there are so many kinds of accrediting agencies around the world. A university may choose not to apply for accreditation at all, apply for one accreditation, or push the envelope to apply for all kinds of accreditation that it can earn. Among the academics, AACSB, EFMD and AMBA are perceived as the world's top accrediting agencies in the field of business education. The term "Triple Crown" is used to refer to those business schools or universities that have been awarded accreditations from all three.

In my opinion, the Triple Crown is just a marketing scheme. As long as a business school has achieved one of these top three accreditations, I think it is pretty good already, meaning that it provides high-quality business programmes and meets international standards. In the next few pages, I will go over these accrediting agencies one-by-one.

AACSB

AACSB stands for "The Association to Advance Collegiate Schools of Business". It was previously known as "The American Assembly of Collegiate Schools of Business". Originally focused on accrediting American business schools, this US-headquartered organization has since expanded to provide accreditation service to over 500 universities in 7 continents. Examples of AACSB-accredited universities include Harvard, UC Berkeley, and Yale.

Some students confuse AACSB membership with accreditation. To be eligible for AACSB accreditation consideration, a university must first become a member. Since AACSB has stringent criteria in accepting members, having AACSB membership is a good sign, but it is not the same as AACSB accreditation. The list of "AACSB accredited universities" can be found here:

https://www.aacsb.net/eweb/DynamicPage.
aspx?Site=AACSB&WebKey=ED088FF2-979E-48C6-B104-
33768F1DE01D

To learn more about AACSB in general, visit its web site at:

http://www.aacsb.edu

AMBA

AMBA stands for "The Association of MBAs". This UK-based organization provides programme-specific accreditation service to over 160 universities in 72 countries. AMBA specializes in accrediting MBA, DBA, and MBM programmes. About 30% of AMBA-accredited universities are located in the United Kingdom with the rest mainly in other parts of Europe. Examples of AMBA-accredited online MBA programmes include many British programmes such as those from Aberdeen, Durham, Henley, Imperial, Leicester, and Warwick. To learn more about AMBA in general, visit its web site at:

http://www.mbaworld.com

EFMD EQUIS & EFMD CEL

EFMD stands for "European Foundation for Management Development". This Belgium-based organization provides accreditation service to hundreds of universities and some consultancy firms. EFMD has several types of accreditation services. The most popular is that designed for brick-and-mortar business schools, called "EQUIS", which stands for "European Quality Improvement System". For online programmes, they may choose to apply for the "CEL" accreditation, which is a programme-specific accreditation for teChnology-Enhanced Learning. Examples of EFMD CEL-accredited programmes include the online MBA from Liverpool and U21Global, and the Master programme from UMUC. To learn more about EFMD in general, visit its web site at:

http://www.efmd.org

Accreditation in Canada

Unlike in the United States, there is no institutional accreditation in Canada. That said, there are still ways to identify the better universities from the group of legitimate ones. If I were you, I would first look at the membership list from the Association of Universities and Colleges of Canada (AUCC):

http://www.aucc.ca/can_uni/our_universities/index_e.html

As pointed out in the AUCC Corporate Brochure, "AUCC members meet a set of criteria for institutional membership that considers academic freedom, depth of program offerings, and a commitment to scholarship and research" (AUCC, 2010, p7.). As such, you can infer that membership in AUCC is the "mark of quality higher education" in Canada.

Having a license issued by the provincial ministry of education to operate as a degree-granting institution does not mean that the institution has achieved accreditation. Again, there's no institutional accreditation system in Canada. To help them further differentiate themselves from others, top Canadian business schools such as Ivy, Queen's, and Rotman would seek international accreditation from AACSB, AMBA and/or EFMD-EQUIS, while other Canadian business schools may seek American accreditation such as that from the Distance Education and Training Council (DETC).

If you are interested in learning more about the ranking of Canadian universities in general, you may consult the annual university ranking as published by *Maclean's* magazine. Although some education experts and business school deans argue that *Maclean's* ranking is not complete and can be biased, I think it serves pretty well as a starting point in your university search. Learn more at:

http://oncampus.macleans.ca/education/rankings

Accreditation in the United States

There are three kinds of accreditations that American universities can seek. These are:

1. Global business accreditation – e.g., AMBA, AACSB, and/or EFMD

2. Regional accreditation – e.g., from one of the six regional accrediting agencies

3. National accreditation – e.g., from DETC, ACBSP, and/or IACBE

Please note that these accreditations are not mutually exclusive, so it is not uncommon to find universities that hold multiple accreditation. The discussion of American degree and accreditation can be biased, subjective, and confusing. If you merely study the information as presented by the various accrediting agencies, you may learn that they are made kind of equally and their respective accredited universities are all good ones. Since my students keep bugging me on this topic, I cannot help but share with you my own opinion. You are strongly advised to do your research and draw your own conclusions, should you find a big difference between what I am going to say and your understanding on this matter.

In my opinion, the best business school holds the AACSB accreditation because it is the most difficult one to obtain. AMBA and EFMD EQUIS/CEL are also good accreditations to have. I would not hesitate to recommend my students to study at a university that holds one or more of these global management-specific accreditations. If the degree is to come from an American university, I would also check to see if it holds regional accreditation. Well-respected universities like Harvard, Northwestern, and Yale all hold regional accreditations so you can draw some inference from that.

How about national accreditations? This is the most controversial part, and my position is that "Having national accreditation is better than having no accreditation at all." I do not have enough information to tell you the difference among the Accreditation Council for Business Schools and Programs (ACBSP), the DETC, and the International Assembly for Collegiate Business Education (IACBE). Just take a look at their lists of accredited universities and you can get some idea about their calibre. That said, Lansbridge University, an online university based in New Brunswick, was re-accredited by DETC only two months prior to being forced to closure by the New Brunswick government in 2010; that should give you some hints about the difference in education standard and expectation across the border.

If you are interested in learning about the ranking of American universities in general, you can consult the annual university ranking as published by the *Bloomberg Businessweek* magazine. Just like the *Maclean's* ranking, some argue that the *Bloomberg Businessweek* ranking is flawed, methodologically speaking. Having said that, it will not hurt to make good use of such ranking to get a general idea about the higher education landscape in the United States. Learn more at:

http://www.businessweek.com/bschools/rankings

Regional Accrediting Agencies

There are six regional accrediting agencies in the United States, and they are all recognized by the USDOE and CHEA. I have listed the web pages in which you can locate the respective accredited universities that are under their supervision:

1. **Middle States Commission on Higher Education:**

   http://www.msche.org/institutions_directory.asp

2. **New England Association of Universities and Colleges – Commission on Institutions of Higher Education:**

   http://cihe.neasc.org/about_our_institutions/roster_of_institutions

3. **North Central Association of Colleges and Universities – The Higher Learning Commission:**

http://www.ncahlc.org/component/option,com_directory/
Itemid,184

4. Northwest Commission on Colleges and Universities:

http://www.nwccu.org/Directory%20of%20Inst/Member%20
Institutions/All%20Institutions.htm

5. Southern Association of Colleges and Universities Commission on Colleges:

http://www.sacscoc.org/searchResults.asp

6. Western Association of Universities and Colleges Accrediting Commission for Senior Colleges and Universities:

http://www.wascsenior.org/directory/institutions

National Accrediting Agencies

In addition to the Triple Crown that I have mentioned earlier in the chapter, three more business accreditations are commonly found in the United States. They are accreditations coming from the ACBSP, DETC, and IACBE. While these accrediting agencies cover universities in other countries as well, most of their accredited programmes are provided by community colleges or smaller universities in the United States. In the academic community, the accreditations given by these three agencies are usually referred to as "national accreditation". For more information, please visit their official web sites:

ACBSP: http://www.acbsp.org

DETC: http://www.detc.org

IACBE: http://www.iacbe.org

Accreditation in the United Kingdom

The term "accreditation" is used differently in the UK. Having an accreditation simply means that the university is authorized by the British government to issue a degree. It does not reflect how good or bad a university is being run, as long as it exceeds the minimum standard as required by law.

To find out which university is better than others, one may need to spend some time going over the "Review Reports" as issued by the Quality Assurance Agency for Higher Education (QAA). The QAA is contracted by the Higher Education Funding Council for England (HEFCE) to assess universities on its behalf:

http://www.qaa.ac.uk/reviews/reports/instindex.asp

There are several ways to find out the general ranking of British universities. Students can consult the *Times Good University Guide, Guardian University Guide, Sunday Times University Guide, The Compete University Guide*, and *The Telegraph University League Table*. One of the most influential rankings is published by the *Financial Times* (FT) newspaper. You can view it online at:

http://rankings.ft.com/businessschoolrankings/rankings

Perhaps the most interesting thing to know is that *Financial Times* also maintains a "listing" (not ranking) of top online business degree providers. Some of them are from the United Kingdom but many are based overseas. You can view such listing by going to:

http://rankings.ft.com/businessschoolrankings/online-mba

Accreditation in Australia

Similar to the situation in the United Kingdom, all degree-granting universities in Australia have received accreditation from the government. Hence, phrases like "accredited online degree from Australia" simply means that it is a degree issued by a legitimate university in Australia, as you cannot (and should not) seek a degree from an "unaccredited" university. To learn about the quality of each university, you need to study the "Quality Audit" report as prepared by The Australian Universities Quality Agency (AUQA):

http://www.auqa.edu.au/qualityaudit/universities

How about ranking? In general, Australians rely on two major rankings for their universities; these are the *Times Higher Education World University Ranking* and the *QS World University Rankings*. The latter can be found here:

http://www.topuniversities.com/university-rankings/world-university-rankings/home

Accreditation Period

If the university you are thinking of applying to has received accreditation from the appropriate accrediting agency, that is good. However, your search is not yet finished. You still need to check two things:

1. Expiration date of the accreditation

2. Status of accreditation

Since accreditation does not last forever once it has been granted, you have to pay special attention to the accreditation period. What if your university's accreditation is going to expire in six months' time? There is still a possibility that your university may not get re-accredited for whatever reasons. Hence, it is best to look for a university that does not need to renew its accreditation for at least two or three years.

Another common issue is the status of accreditation. Some universities may have received a "conditional pass" on accreditation based on the assumption that certain deficiencies (e.g., in curriculum design or faculty recruitment) will be addressed by a certain timeframe. As a result, it is to your best interest to study the accreditation or audit report about the university. If the report is unfavorable, it is best to look for another university even if it has already been accredited. Why take the risk?

Accreditation Mill Scam

If a criminal can set up a fake university, how hard can it be to create a fake accrediting agency to give the fake university proper accreditation? In recent years, I have observed a proliferation of fake accrediting agencies popping up on the net. To help you avoid these accreditation mills, I am going to list "some" of the well-known troublemakers here. Please note that new accreditation mills appear everyday, so you are strongly urged to use common sense in your judgment because the following list may become outdated soon:

Accelerated Degree Programs

Accrediting Commission International

American Association of International Medical Graduates

Association for Online Academic Excellence

Association of Christian Colleges and Theological Universities

Central States Council on Distance Education

Distance Graduation Accrediting Association

Distance Learning Council of Europe

Education Accreditation Association

European Accreditation Board of Higher Education Universities

European Council for Distance & Open Learning

Expressive Psychology Association

International Association of Universities and Universities

International DETC

iDETC

International Education Ministry of Accreditation Association

International University Accrediting Association

National Board of Education

Southern Accrediting Association of Bible Institutes and Colleges

United Congress of Colleges Ireland, UK

US-DETC

Virtual University Accrediting Association

World Association of Universities and Colleges

World Council For Excellence in Higher Education

Once again, these are fake accreditation agencies. So, if the university you are planning to apply to has any affiliation with these entities, run!

Chapter 8 - DBA and PhD

Life After MBA

The MBA degree seemed to be the golden passport to enter senior management rank during the 1970s and the 1980s, but how about today? In North America, more and more people have gained access to graduate management studies in the last two decades, so it is not uncommon to find many of your colleagues in the middle management level armed with an MBA degree. To seek a better career perspective, some will go for a professional designation in a specialized field such as CA, CMA, or CGA in the accounting area, while others may improve their skills in project management with the PMP designation. For those who like to sharpen their leadership skills, the Sloan program at London Business School, MIT, and Stanford are also good choices if you are willing to spend a year or two to study abroad.

In the past, not many people thought of pursuing a doctorate degree in business. This is because unless you are working in a university, a policy think-tank, or a research-oriented government agency, few PhDs are working in the industry. Not sure if you have heard this joke, but some people see a PhD as a degree that may cause "Permanent Head Damage" or at least some hair loss! However, the whole education landscape has changed in the last decade when the MBA degree has started to become a commodity, and new online DBA and PhD programmes are proliferating in the market. So, what exactly are these terminal business degrees? Let me spend a few minutes to discuss them in the next few pages.

PhD

PhD stands for Doctor of Philosophy. This academic doctorate is the terminal (i.e., highest) degree that most people would get. Technically speaking, my statement is incorrect because there is still the Doctor of Letters (D.Litt.), which is a higher doctorate above PhD. However, because the D.Litt. is rare in reality, just consider the PhD as the highest degree for our discussion. In the business field, the PhD degree may come in the name of "PhD in Management", "PhD in Business Administration", or just "PhD in Administration". They are all highly similar in terms of curriculum. PhD students usually spend 40% in coursework (i.e., attending lectures) and 60% on research. It is not uncommon for PhD students to spend up to five or six years of full-time study to complete their dissertation of 50,000+ words and eventually receive the blessing from the PhD supervisor and the defence committee.

DBA

Traditionally, a PhD degree is all you can seek when pursuing a doctoral business degree. The situation has changed since the mid-2000s when British and Australian universities flooded the education market with a wide variety of DBA programmes for business executives. DBA stands for Doctor of Business Administration. This professional doctorate is also a terminal degree in the field of business. Please note that the DBA is not a new invention; this degree has been offered for years at elite schools like Harvard. Relatively speaking, the DBA is not as common as the PhD, so don't be alarmed if someone accidentally mixes up your prestigious doctor of business administration degree with "database administrator" title in the IT field because both share the same "DBA" designation.

In terms of curriculum, DBA students would typically spend 60% of the time on coursework and the rest in conducting research and dissertation writing. The required word count for a DBA dissertation is slightly lower than that of a PhD, in the range of 35,000 to 45,000 words. Depending on the university, an external review of the DBA dissertation by a panel of examiners may be used in lieu of a verbal defence. Many DBA students would complete their programme on a part-time basis while still working in their organizations. Because of that, the duration of study varies significantly; it ranges from two and a half years for a fast learner all the way up to six or seven years for a super-busy executive.

If you are still confused about the two terminal business degrees, think of a PhD as a degree for developing a "professional researcher" whereas a DBA is one for developing a "research professional". Regardless of whether you are pursuing a PhD or a DBA, you are the "Dr." in your field.

5 Myths About DBAs

Myth #1: A DBA graduate is not qualified to be a professor because universities only hire PhDs.

Fact: This is simply untrue. Government agencies around the world have stated clearly that they consider a DBA degree as equivalent to a PhD degree academically speaking. Holders of both degrees can use the "Dr." title. Do not forget that top schools like Harvard Business School also run a DBA programme. Perhaps a more accurate statement should be "A PhD or DBA holder who has completed his or her degree from a lower-tier university may not easily get a teaching job at a tier-1 university."

Myth #2: A DBA graduate is not qualified to submit journal papers

Fact: This is also untrue. The fact is that anybody can submit manuscript to a journal for consideration, regardless of whether he or she has a high school diploma, an undergraduate degree, a master's degree, or a terminal one. Of course, you need to conduct proper research and have the ability to write a decent journal article to get accepted for publication. There are no rules and regulations that restrict DBA students or graduates from submitting manuscript to any academic journal.

Myth #3: A DBA programme is easy to complete

Fact: The dropout rate of a DBA programme is similar to that of a PhD. While the percentage of coursework is relatively higher than that of a PhD (60% vs. 40%), don't forget that a DBA student still needs to conduct high-quality research, write the "yellow page" (the nick name of a thick DBA dissertation), and get the approval of the DBA supervisor and external examiners. Furthermore, most DBAs are part-timers, making it even more challenging to complete the study when juggling among family, work, and study priorities.

Myth #4: A DBA programme is less expensive

Fact: This may not be true for two reasons. First of all, most DBA programmes are full cost-recovery programmes that are not subsidized by the government. Hence, in most cases it will not be cheaper than a PhD programme. Furthermore, the amount that you pay is often determined by the length of your study. Let's say your original plan is to complete the research and dissertation phase in two years' time, but you eventually end up spending five years for that. In this case, you still have to pay the university extra fees to cover the extra three years of supervision time by your professor, even when there is no physical or online class to attend.

Myth #5: DBA students are younger

Fact: This is not true and the opposite is often observed. This is because many DBA students are working professionals who had obtained their MBA degrees earlier. As a result, you may come across DBA students in the 35-50 years age group who are holding middle to senior management roles in their organizations.

List of 100% Online DBA and PhD Programmes

Since quite a number of my MBA students wish to pursue online doctoral business degree, I have prepared the following list for their reference. Please note that it is not a comprehensive list and it is also not a ranking. After all, you need to consider your objectives, the programme's pedagogy and reputation, and the amount of tuition fee that you can afford when evaluating these universities. I am listing those programmes that can be done remotely from Canada, meaning there is no need to leave your job or relocate to another city in order to pursue your study.

Here is the list in alphabetical order:

Aston University, UK (AACSB-accredited)

Programme: Executive DBA

Web Site: http://www1.aston.ac.uk/aston-business-school/
programmes/research/the-aston-dba/flexible-and-distance-learning

Heriot-Watt University, UK

Programme: DBA

Web Site: http://www.postgraduate.hw.ac.uk/course/210

University of Liverpool, UK

Programme: DBA

Web Site: http://www.liv.ac.uk/study/postgraduate/taught_
courses/laureate_online_doctorate_business_administration.htm

University of Manchester, UK (AACSB-accredited)

Programme: DBA

Web Site: http://www.mbs.ac.uk/postgraduateresearch/
degreetypes/dba/index.aspx

University of Newcastle, Australia

Programme: DBA

Web Site: http://www.gradschool.com.au/Programs/Business--
Marketing/DoctorofBusinessAdministration

University of Reading, UK (AACSB-accredited)

Programme: Henley DBA

Web Site: http://www.henley.reading.ac.uk/management/pg-
research/mgmt-doctor-of-business-administration-dba.aspx

List of DBA and PhD Programmes With Short Residency Requirement

In addition to the 100% online business doctoral degree programmes that I have listed, you can also consider those programmes that have short residency requirement. Actually, it may not be a bad idea to spend just a week or two per year to attend some face-to-face seminars with your fellow classmates and professors. Frankly speaking, I see good value in attending these seminars because it gives you the opportunity to build better relationship with your potential DBA/PhD supervisor. You can also use these workshops to sharpen your skills in statistics and finalize your research design.

Athabasca University, Canada

Programme: DBA

Web site: http://www.mba.athabascau.ca/titanweb/au/webcms. nsf/AllDoc/7A83B7140388E99587256E13005DD5C6?Opendo cument

Case Western Reserve University, USA (AACSB accredited)

Programme: DM (Doctor of Management)

Web site: http://weatherhead.case.edu/academics/doctorate/ management/doctor-of-management.cfm

Grenoble Ecole de Management, France (AACSB and AMBA accredited)

Programme: DBA

Web site: http://www.grenoble-em.com/461-grenoble-ecole-de-management-dba-program-2.aspx

Nova Southeastern University, USA

Programme: DBA

Web site: http://www.huizenga.nova.edu/FutureStudents/
Doctoral/DBA.cfm

Royal Roads University, Canada*

Programme: DBA

Web site: http://business.school.royalroads.ca

*Special note: As of this writing (Dec 2010), Royal Roads has
not yet officially launched its distance learning DBA programme,
despite its intention to do so since 2005. I am listing it here in
case you are interested in following up with the Royal Roads DBA
development, if any.

University of Maryland University College, USA

Programme: DM (Doctor of Management)

Web site: http://www.umuc.edu/doctor

Chapter 9 - The Ideal Place to Study

My Cubicle?

Thinking of studying in your own cubicle? Forget it. It is not going to work because your desk phone will keep ringing, e-mail will keep arriving in your Outlook, and your lovely neighbours who are staying late in the office will come to bug you for chitchat. All of these make it virtually impossible for you to concentrate on your study.

When I was doing my doctoral study in early 2000s, I was working at the headquarters of a national telecommunications provider. I was staying late at 6pm to do some quiet study in my own cubicle, and my boss' boss came to me and said, "Ken, I don't mind you to study but please don't use company resources for it. When you are in the office, you should be working and not studying. It's 6pm alright so why don't you leave the office now?" Frankly speaking, I was astonished. The next day I consulted my HR people upstairs. It turned out that while there was no company policy that prevented me from studying online using company equipment in my own cubicle, the fact that I was staying late was creating trouble for my boss' boss. This was because he had to stay late as well to ensure the floor's security and assure my personal safety.

Alright, I compromised. After saying goodbye to my colleagues on the floor at about 5:30pm every day, I left the company's building premises and walked to a nearby coffee shop to begin my daily online study. That is how I found the best place to study – a coffee shop.

Coffee Shop with Free Internet Access

The year 2010 was a great year for high-tech gadget owners. You could now find free Wi-Fi Internet access in virtually all of the major coffee chains in Canada: Second Cup, Starbucks, and Bridgehead. To use the free Wi-Fi at Second Cup, a one-time online account registration is all you need. Then, every time you want to access the Internet, just open your web browser that will automatically point you to the Wi-Fi access landing page. Then, click the "Second Cup Account" logo to enter your e-mail address and password to gain Internet access. I believe Second Cup gives you a free two-hour access for every successful log-in.

To use the free Wi-Fi service at Starbucks, you do not need any account registration. Simply open your web browser to see the Wi-Fi landing page, then click the check box to accept the terms and agreement. In a matter of seconds, you will be connected to the Internet. This used to be a charged service, but Bell Canada has entered into an agreement with Starbucks to provide free service starting in summer 2010. I don't think there is any time limit for your Wi-Fi usage at Starbucks.

If you reside in Ottawa, you know the Bridgehead chain is "The" popular place for organic coffee in the city. To use the free Wi-Fi service at Bridgehead, you need to first get a voucher from the cashier when you buy your coffee or muffin. This voucher will show you the temporary access code and password for your one-hour free Internet access. In some smaller Bridgehead stores you don't need a voucher as they just open up the Wi-Fi for public access.

If you reside in a location where the above coffee chains are not available, you may want to check out the following site to find out which local coffee shops and restaurants provide free Wi-Fi Internet access to the public:

http://www.wififreespot.com/can.html

Other locations that are well known for getting free Wi-Fi access include public libraries and hotel lobbies. No matter where you are using the Wi-Fi service, make sure you have carefully selected the correct Wi-Fi access point for Internet access. This is because your location may be covered by several unknown-yet-risky Wi-Fi access points. Take five seconds to confirm the name of your Wi-Fi access point in your computer's networking control panel to ensure you are connecting to the right network. Never connect to an access point that is "device"-based because you may be connecting to the Internet via a hacker's laptop that is located nearby!

Study Anywhere with Mobile Broadband Service

One of the best investments I have ever made is a monthly subscription to my wireless carrier's mobile broadband service. Virtually all of the national wireless carriers (e.g., Bell, TELUS, and Rogers), regional carriers (e.g., Videotron, Sasktel), and the new AWS wireless entrants (e.g., WindMobile and Mobilicity) provide 3G broadband Internet access for your laptop. In terms of equipment, you need to first purchase a 3G adapter from the wireless carrier. It comes in many forms and shape such as USB stick and PCMCIA card. This 3G adapter costs about $99 and you may even get it for free if you sign a multi-year contract with the wireless carrier. There is no need to get those with speeds of 42Mbps or higher because the typical throughput (speed) that you can get in Canada is about 4 to 6Mbps, despite the advertising claims. As a heavy Internet user who is often travelling on the road, I found myself using 500MB to 1GB data per month and I pay $40 to my wireless carrier per month before tax.

Perhaps you may be wondering why I call such an expensive service fee a good investment, especially when people already have access to high-speed Internet at home, in the office, or at many coffee shops. The beauty of this mobile broadband service is that I can connect my laptop to the Internet whenever there is a cellphone signal. This means I can study online when I am taking a 30-minute break in a service station on Hwy 401, having a 5-hour train ride on VIA Rail between Toronto and Ottawa, or waiting for flight departure near the gate in the airport. Another advantage is that it serves as my back-up Internet connectivity. I actually had an incident in which my home's broadband Internet service went down during my examination period. Do you really want to grab your laptop and go to a nearby coffee shop to do your important final exam online at night? I don't think so. My 3G service saved me from the trouble during that Internet outage! Speaking of Internet redundancy, here is another tip that you should consider. Try to get your 3G mobile service from a carrier that is different from your home Internet service provider. For example, if you are using Rogers Cable for Internet at home, get a 3G service from Bell or TELUS. This is because if a carrier's DNS service is down, you can't get access to the Internet no matter you are using their cable network or the wireless one. While DNS service outage does not happen often, it did affect me twice in the last few years especially late at night, so there is still such a possibility. Build your network redundancy as much as possible.

But what if you already have 3G service in your smartphone or iPad? Should you still spend the extra bucks on the 3G stick? Unfortunately, most of the online learning platforms such as Moodle, WebCT, and Blackboard cannot be used properly with these latest hi-tech mobile gadgets. I have heard that Blackboard has just launched a Mobile app to allow iPhone users to surf their online classroom on the phone, but trust me, you will not be too satisfied with the reduced set of functions. Just stick to your laptop. If you are really on a tight budget and already have 3G data on your Nokia or Windows Mobile smartphone, you can consider using a software called JoikuSpot (www.joiku.com) to turn your phone into a temporary Wi-Fi access point for your laptop. In my opinion, however, this is not a sustainable solution because such a setup prevents you from receiving calls during a Wi-Fi access session, plus such usage consumes your smartphone's battery very quickly. You can give it a try and your result may vary.

Epilogue

I hope you have enjoyed reading this book and found it useful. As I write this epilogue, I am sitting in the middle of a shopping mall food court. Many people are buying fast food and there are several long queues. To these hungry shoppers, fast food seems to be the "best" option for them because it is affordable and can be served quickly, even though the food may not have the best taste. After all, it does not make too much sense to ask these busy shoppers to spend an hour or so in an upscale restaurant for fine dining.

I guess the same analogy can be used to analyze online education. Some students have a limited budget for studying while others have time constraints and/or family priorities to deal with. Hence, online education can be the "best" study option for them. As a professor who has taught MBA at a tier-1 business school in Europe, I know how great it can be to study in a beautiful university campus, and to socialize with classmates over drinks after class. However, the fact is that not everybody can afford to quit their full-time job and leave their significant ones behind to purse their dream MBA. My point is that you should pursue an MBA or DBA programme that best fits your needs. Online education is not for everybody, but it can be a great one for those who feel comfortable with such asynchronous mode of learning.

The old saying in the service industry that a consumer can only pick two out of "speed", "price", and "quality" can be applied to online education. A reputable online MBA degree that only costs $3000 and takes only a few months to complete simply does not exist. My advice? Be realistic about your expectations when choosing your online programme. If something sounds too good to be true, it probably is! Just remember there is no shortcut to success. After reading this book, I hope you are in a better position to choose the right degree to pursue, and make more bucks annually.

To those who are browsing this book right now at Chapters/Indigo, just pay for it and evaluate the book leisurely at home for two weeks. Do not stand in the aisle for the whole afternoon! Remember to keep your original receipt if you intend to get a full refund at the bookstore later.

If you have purchased this book as part of Dr. Wong's course, thank you. I hope this little book can make your e-learning journey more enjoyable. If you have just downloaded this book from those illegal websites and would like to keep it on your computer for future reference, you have three options:

1. Go to iUniverse's official web site to purchase a legitimate electronic copy. I have intentionally made the e-book version affordable (about US$10) so that my students can enjoy it without costing them an arm and a leg. Helping you to understand the concept of intellectual properties is one of my teaching objectives.

2. Make a donation to your local charity or become a volunteer. I really mean it. If you absolutely don't want to pay the publisher for whatever reasons, please at least make a difference to help other people in your community.

3. Do nothing, if you think stealing is the right thing to do.

Have a great day and thanks for taking time to read my work.

Cheers,

Ken

References

Accredited and Non-Accredited Colleges and Universities (2011). *Maine Higher Education.* Retrieved from http://www.maine.gov/education/highered/Non-Accredited/non-accredited.htm#DL

Advanced Education (2011). *Department of Education.* Retrieved from http://www.education.gov.yk.ca/advanceded

AUCC (2010). *Speaking for Canada's Universities.* Ottawa, ON: Association of Universities and Colleges of Canada. Retrieved from http://www.aucc.ca/_pdf/english/publications/corp_brochure_e.pdf

AUQA Audit Reports: Universities (2011). *Australian Universities Quality Agency.* Retrieved from http://www.auqa.edu.au/qualityaudit/universities

Business Education (2011). *Financial Times.* Retrieved from http://rankings.ft.com/businessschoolrankings/rankings

Business School Rankings and Profiles (2011). *Bloomberg Businessweek.* Retrieved from http://www.businessweek.com/bschools/rankings

Canadian universities (2011). *Association of Universities and Colleges of Canada*. Retrieved from http://www.aucc.ca/can_uni/our_universities/index_e.html

Colleges and Universities Not Accredited by CHEA (2011). *Michigan Civil Service Commission*. Retrieved from http://www.michigan.gov/documents/Non-accreditedSchools_78090_7.pdf

Database of Institutions and Programs Accredited by Recognized United States Accrediting Organizations (2011). *Council for Higher Education Accreditation*. Retrieved from http://www.chea.org/search/default.asp

Degree Authorization (2011). *Ministry of Advanced Education and Labour Market Development*. Retrieved from http://www.aved.gov.bc.ca/degree-authorization/applicants.htm

Directory of Universities, Colleges and Schools in the Provinces and Territories of Canada (2011). *Canadian Information Centre for International Credentials*. Retrieved from http://www.cicic.ca/664/directory-of-universities-colleges-and-universities-in-canada.canada

ECE Home (2011). *Ministry of Education, Culture and Employment*. Retrieved from http://www.ece.gov.nt.ca

Formation universitaire (2011). *Ministère de l'Éducation*. Retrieved from http://www.mels.gouv.qc.ca/sections/demandeAdmission/index.asp?page=universitaire

Free Wi-Fi Canada (2011). *Wi-Fi Free Spot*. Retrieved from http://www.wififreespot.com/can.html

Higher education providers (2011). *Department of Education, Employment and Workplace Relations.* Retrieved from http://www.goingtouni.gov.au/Main/CoursesAndProviders/ProvidersAndCourses/HigherEducationProviders/Default.htm

Institution Search (2011). *U.S. Department of Education.* Retrieved from http://ope.ed.gov/accreditation/Search.aspx

Island Information: Universities and Colleges (2011). *The Government of Prince Edward Island.* Retrieved from http://www.gov.pe.ca/infopei/index.php3?number=787&lang=E

Online Learning Cost Savings Calculator (2011). *The SUNY Learning Network.* Retrieved from http://sln.suny.edu/gs/gs_costcalculator.shtml

Overview (2011). *CourseSmart.* Retrieved from http://www.coursesmart.com/overview

Post-Secondary Educational Institutions (2011). *Ministry of Advanced Education, Employment and Immigration.* Retrieved from http://www.aeel.gov.sk.ca/post-secondary-educ-Institutions

Post-Secondary Education - Universities (2011). *Ministry of Manitoba Advanced Education and Literacy.* Retrieved from http://www.edu.gov.mb.ca/ael/unicoll/universities.html

Post-Secondary Institutions in New Brunswick (2011). *Department of Post-Secondary Education, Training and Labour.* Retrieved from http://www.gnb.ca/0105/ps/univ_ccnb-e.asp

Programmes We Accredit (2011). *Association of MBAs*. Retrieved from http://www.mbaworld.com/index.php?option=com_content&view=a rticle&id=432&Itemid=132

Programs - Listed by Provider (2011). *Canadian Virtual University*. Retrieved from http://www.cvu-uvc.ca/cgi-bin/cvu/cvuinfo. cgi?qn=institution&lang=en

Public Institutions (2011). *Department of Education*. Retrieved from http://www.ed.gov.nl.ca/edu/postsecondary/public.html

Publicly Funded Institutions (2011). *Ministry of Alberta Advanced Education and Technology*. Retrieved from http://www. advancededucation.gov.ab.ca/post-secondary/institutions/public.aspx

QS World University Rankings (2011). *QS-TopUniversities*. Retrieved from http://www.topuniversities.com/university-rankings/world-university-rankings/home

Recognized Bodies Search (2011). *BIS-Department for Business Innovation & Skills*. Retrieved from http://www.dcsf.gov.uk/ recognisedukdegrees/index.cfm?fuseaction=institutes.list&InstituteCa tegoryID=1&OrderBy=Category

Review Report (2011). *Quality Assurance Agency*. Retrieved from http://www.qaa.ac.uk/reviews/reports/instindex.asp

Schools Accredited in Business (2011). *The Association to Advance Collegiate Schools of Business*. Retrieved from https://www.aacsb.net/

eweb/DynamicPage.aspx?Site=AACSB&WebKey=ED088FF2-979E-48C6-B104-33768F1DE01D

School Services (2011). *Department of Education.* Retrieved from http://www.edu.gov.nu.ca/apps/authoring/dspPage.aspx?page=47

Tuition Tax Credit - Educational Institutions Outside Canada (2011). *Canada Revenue Agency.* Retrieved from http://www.cra-arc.gc.ca/E/pub/tp/it516r2/it516r2-e.html#P71_6821

Unaccredited colleges (2011). *Oregon Student Assistance Commission Office of Degree Authorization.* Retrieved from http://www.osac.state.or.us/oda/unaccredited.aspx

Universities (2011). *Ministry of Training, Colleges and Universities.* Retrieved from http://www.tcu.gov.on.ca/eng/postsecondary/schoolsprograms/university/index.html

Universities & College (2011). *Department of Education.* Retrieved from http://www.ednet.ns.ca/contact/universities.shtml

University Rankings (2011). *Macleans.* Retrieved from http://oncampus.macleans.ca/education/rankings

What is EQUIS? (2011). *EFMD.* Retrieved from http://www.efmd.org/index.php/accreditation-/equis/what-is-equis

Index

A

AACSB x, xiv, 8, 22, 51, 52, 53, 55, 56, 68, 69, 70, 85
ACBSP 55, 56, 58, 59
Accreditation x, xi, 47, 48, 51, 54, 55, 56, 59, 60, 61, 62, 82
Admission x, 26, 28
Alberta 44, 84
AMBA x, 9, 22, 52, 53, 55, 56, 70
American Government x, 47
AUCC 54, 55, 81
AUQA 60, 81
Australian Government x, 50

B

Blackboard 18, 75
Bloomberg Businessweek 21, 57, 81
British Columbia 42, 44
British Government x, 49

C

Canadian Government x, 42
Canadian Virtual University 1, 84
CEL x, xiv, 3, 54, 56
CGPA 28
CHEA x, 40, 47, 57, 82
CO2 emissions 2
Content-enhanced Programme ix, 17
Cost Savings Calculator 2, 83
CourseNet 18

D

DBA iii, iv, xi, xv, xviii, 6, 22, 23, 53, 64, 65, 66, 67, 68, 69, 70, 71, 77

Degree-Granting Authority x, 20
Desire2Learn 18
DETC 55, 56, 58, 59, 62
Diploma Mills x, 35, 36, 48
Discussion Board–based programme 13

E

e-book 30, 78
Eco-friendly ix, 2
EFMD x, xiv, 3, 9, 22, 52, 54, 55, 56, 85
EQUIS x, 54, 55, 56, 85

F

Facebook ix, xiv, xv, 13, 17
Financial Times 3, 21, 59, 81
First Class 18

G

GMAT 26, 28

H

HEFCE 59

I

IACBE 55, 56, 58, 59

J

Job Promotion ix, 8

L

Learning Management System ix, 18
Legitimate Universities x, 42
LMS 16, 17, 18, 32, 34